On
Waking Up
All Over The
World

Paul Paparella

On
Waking Up
All Over The
World

Paul Paparella

Distinction Poets
Waitsfield, Vermont

On Waking Up All Over the World
by Paul Paparella

Published by   Distinction Press
PO Box 876
Waitsfield, Vermont 05673
www.distinctionpress.com

Author Photograph: Justin Frawley
Cover Photograph: Kitty Werner
Back Cover Photograph: Kitty Werner
Design & Typesetting: Kitty Werner, Distinction Press

To contact Paul Paparella for readings or workshops:

Paul Paparella
127 Covey Road
Westford, Vermont 05494
PPaparella@aol.com

ISBN 978-0-9802175-1-3
Printed in the USA

Acknowledgments
Grateful acknowledgment is made to the editors of the publications in which these poems first appeared, some in slightly different forms.

Buffalo Carp: "A Barn at Twilight"
Educational Leadership: "They Are Your Children. And Mine"
The Middle School Journal: "They Are Your Children. And Mine"
Audacious Poetry: Reflections of Adolescence: "They Are Your Children. And Mine"
Iowa State University: Video Tape: "They Are All Our Children"
Off the Coast: "Life on the Second Floor"
Quoin: "The City"
Red Horse Hill: "Rushing Things"
The Teachers Voice: "Attention Deficit Disorder," "Peter"
Willard & Maple XI: "Garage Sale," "Snow Hare"

For my wife, Cathy, for believing in me
and for our children,
Peggy, Nancy, Beth, and Paul
for their constant love and support

For Kitty Werner, who made it happen

The author is grateful that the publication of
this book is supported by a
Literary Grant from
John and Katherine Paterson

The Poems

Two Old Friends

The other day two old friends ambled up to my
door, onomatopoeia and personification, one
tapping insistently, the other an amorphous lump,
to ask me why I had not used them of late,
at least consciously.

I said I had gotten away from the fundamental
differences between the literal and the figurative
and had settled into a language incorporating
both. Sort of a hybrid without an attempt to
even the score or favor one over the other.
I could not even define such a style. They
should not take it personally.

Onomatopoeia beat open the door, personification
gave voice to a slithering, sliding snake alliterating
in the hallway. Both took my apology personally.

I knew they were assembling all of their
poetic figures of speech. Metaphor and simile
feverishly compared notes. Rhyme could not be
far behind and the marching feet of the Anapestic, the
Dactylic, the Trochaic, and the Iambic Pentameter
limped over the landscape.

I was outnumbered, literally and figuratively,
and decided on the spot to try my hand at prose,
the short story and the novel, beckoning me to
a life of adjectives and adverbs, description,
stories, and characters who would not talk back,
or at least I hoped so.

Poetry Reading in Autumn

I have traveled the requisite fifty miles,
to a leafy campus to read my poems to
students required to attend.
And to some lovers of my poetry who have
read my other book, comfortable in their
bed or perhaps on a bench in a park or
sitting in a stuffed chair in Barnes and
Noble, sipping coffee, slowly, deep
within the cadence of one of my poems.

Fifty miles east my students must write a
sonnet and wonder what that has to do with
anything anyway. Some wonder whether I
will really count the fourteen lines and
question why not fifteen or twenty.
Others resent the awful juxtaposition
between choosing Ultimate Frisbee and an art
form long past its time.

I insist that the couplet has to fit like a cornerstone,
The cement tamped down, all edges smooth.

A Barn at Twilight

Each night in my car on Rt. 128, I take a snapshot,
the barn door open, a falling sunset behind my back,
and I watch a single fan blow twilight out of windows
and doors and night enter like a flame gone out.

In their nightly ritual, the cows in single file, gridlock
in the entrance way, a ninety degree turn working its
will upon them.

They work their jaws as if in conversation,
their heads bent in their perpetual meal, the melancholy
light from energy-saving bulbs graying their black and
white skin.

Their stapled red tags hang like costumed jewelry from
their ears. I imagine them slow-dancing on the damp straw.
A branding iron and an empty pail hang like rust from a
wooden beam. In lagoons below, waste gathers.

Heifers disappear into the dark of their private rooms.
A giant blue silo spreads its shadows across the barn
like a moving sentinel. It follows me to the right turn
onto Cambridge Road and retreats back to its post.

Later as I examine my time lapsed photography, I see
no two days the same, no two twilights the same, no two
nights the same, but enough things the same to proclaim
a theory of cowness, to warrant more snapshots in the
hope of detecting a touch of vanity when I look into their
seemingly vacuous eyes balanced by two red tags dangling
from their ears.

On Waving to an Amish Lady

She came out of a bonnet,
out of the wheat,
out of herself,
for a brief, indescribable
moment.
She hesitated and then
raised her hand to me
waving through glass,
my side mirror framing her,
freezing her child-like wave,
fingers opening and closing,
birds bursting from the stone wall of a barn
at each unfolding,
the signal of release, the creation of a new person,
my wave breaking glass to her, hers in my glass mirror,
from side to overhead and smaller now and gone,
except that she and I will never again be the same.

Rushing Things

I watched the weather grow outside
and every living thing surrender to it.

The ghost which moved the dried hay
around in circles pushed the childrens'
swing and it twisted and jiggled like a
puppet gone mad.

And the moon looked for cover behind
clouds which moved across the sky and
fell off the edge of the earth.

The hay and swing and moon were out of
season and the sun sent sputtering rays to
the artificial plant on the window ledge.

I reached for the watering can and poured
life on plastic leaves.

Snow Hare

The bullet limped a little on the wind
and he carried it half in, half out of
his body like cold.
He remembered the barbed-wire fence,
the blood drying up when the wind
pressed the raking wound shut.

Now surrender worked its way up his legs.
A pulse of life opened him and he bled again,
like tears.
He turned and followed the scent for food,
caught in the depth of his own footsteps,
sinking below vision, caught in the frenzy
of his own blood, staining the snow for as
far as the eye could see.

Peter

Peter walked, dragging the sidewalk behind,
he climbed ramps at a precipitous angle,
a tortuous foot at a time,
his legs drained of blood,
his muscles turning to sponge,
while the $75,000 elevator built for him
with the padded walls from top to bottom,
hung like a bell in its shaft,
an artifact for the ages.

Peter walked, dragging the sidewalk behind,
never asked by school officials if he wanted an
elevator. The key dangling like a talisman around
his neck.

Peter chose to be tied to earth,
hanging on when it tilted,
his journey measured in half steps,
his will expressed inches at a time.

To Thine Own Self Be True

Carl: Did you know, Evelyn, that some people are bores all their lives? Did you know that, Evelyn, did you?

Evelyn: Yes.

Carl: They go through life boring people to death. The question is, do they bore themselves?

Evelyn: Apparently not.

Carl: Have you known any bores, Evelyn?

Evelyn: Yes.

Carl: You have? Recently or all of your life?

Evelyn: More recently.

Chess with Myself

The knights were making God-awful noises,
the bishops were proselytizing all over the
board,
the rooks were heat-seeking missiles,
the pawns were tilting and falling over each
other, all sworn to protect the king,
the queens in their haughty grandeur, moved
among and above the din,
an historical perspective their only shield.
The kings one-stepped themselves to the edge
of the melee,
victory danced like a returning mistress,
defeat slouched like the last light before dark.

I move quickly from position to position,
stopping the flow of sand in the minute glass,
an antiseptic montage of dust, blood, and death
overwhelms my senses and I am ready for lunch.

I will find my quiet time even if I have to resort
to checkmate.

The French and Indian War

I wish someone had taught me about the French and
    Indian War.
Or about Napoleon or the Van Allen Belt. Or about
    meiosis.
Or about primogeniture. Or about the Heisenberg
    uncertainty
principle. Much less about Werner Heisenberg. I could
    go on for
decades with the things I wish someone had taught me. I
    just might.

Amicus curiae and in situ come to mind. As does
    Manumission.
And covalent bond. Sang Froid is surely something
I should know. Just on the tip of my tongue sit, with their
    legs
crossed, Sancho Panza, Charles Sanders Pierce, and Lord
    Kelvin.
During recess, ladies like Cassandra, Mary Cassatt, and
    Patricia
Graham swing just out of my reach while Brisbane sits
    waiting
for me to find a match for him on today's quiz.

Warp and woof seem to go together and patient Penelope
waits for what? Antoine Lavoisier and Bosporus are ten
    across and
five down in a puzzle completed in ink. M. M. Guxman
    and Einar
Haugen are kin through an alphabetical listing, by
    columns, of things
an educated man should know. T. Trabasso and James
    Trefil look

forlornly across the page at Mason Weems who sits
   sandwiched
between Webster's Dictionary and Oscar Wilde.

I challenge someone in a game of Scrabble to find xylem
   in the
dictionary. He smiles at my ignorance and adds 67
   points to his
score while I ponder a two-letter word starting with Q
   and ending
with Z.

The Dorm Room

In dorm room 223, a stuffed hibernating

bear slumbers at the foot of her bed,

sleepily eyeing a stuffed yellow snake coiled

amorously around a lamp, its crossed-eyes

focused intently upon its slitted red tongue.

The animals now exist in a world of benign neglect,

cotton spilling from their sides after years

of bouncing around the dryer.

A screen saver lights a corner of the room,

family messages pulsate in the red glow

of a phone, a fan hums in another corner,

and the coiled snake slides off her roommate's

lamp to the floor.

A turning foot pushes the bear off the bed,

where it lies rump up, face down, in its sleep.

The valedictorian and the salutatorian will attend classes tomorrow and meet for lunch. They have survived the ice breakers and will ride the melt leading to friendship or enmity.

Last Christmas

A window on the fourth floor opens like an eye.
I am holding my father around the waist,
as he pushes our Christmas tree out the window,
needles through the eye, tinsel sailing like
silver fish, landing with a soft bounce,
or skipping along upright, kingly and down.

The trees with needles falling off made the
best fires; the needles pricked your finger through
the gloves and you licked the blood away.
In the heat, your face melted and the buildings
and your friends.

Your innocence sniffed like a stray dog
at the pyre; it was your last Christmas.
Your bone-chilled body could have
told you that.

Vietnam Remembered

Burrowing animals sniffed fire
and the smell of flesh and
picked their way over bodies
and rags and digging tools
without handles;

They pawed at a wickless candle
resting on a table without legs
and it rolled away in the dark.
They lay evolutionary claim to
the twists and turns in the tunnel
and tended to housekeeping as
though they had never been
interrupted;

A grenade lay in the corner,
spilling out powder like a
prehistoric egg.

Creativity

Much of the great art of the world
was done by candlelight.
A sobering thought to us who bask
in electricity.

The first flame that drew oxygen's
breath was a prelude to great art.

The first artists, unaccustomed to an
orgy of light, reproduced animals they
hunted on the walls of their cave like
20th century movies. Their families
etched their history through torch light.

For centuries a symphony of sporadic
light accompanied the artist.
Candlelight, left to the whims of the wind
played its ghost-like tricks upon the canvas.

The moon mimicked daylight, becoming
more intrusive as the wicks labored and
the flames burned brightest in the floating
wax. The painter had to catch the perfect
moment of light, daylight and candlelight
battling for supremacy.

The musician focused upon notes rising in
the air, the melody filtering down to cool
by his side.
Dancers entered from the wings, their
shadows rising like giants.

The writer dipped his pen to the movement
of candlelight, following living language

in its evolutionary journey, through
millennia of time, carried by the wind and
marauding armies.
Mere words rising from the ashes, smoke
between his fingers as he moves the
flambeau, giving life to the storyteller in
word and song.

The transcriber did the heavy lifting,
deciphering language from many hands,
preserving genius while smoke poked at the
ceiling with a gentle taunt, looking to escape
with language for a new century.

The Return of the Realm

The
Wise
Men
Have
Been
Beheaded.

They
Stand
In
Their
Chalk
Dust,

Cradling
Their
Gifts,

Nimbly
Stepping
Over
Their
Heads,

In
The
Practiced
Art
Of
Kings.

First Born

Inside carrying fire in my hand,
flashing heat from my eyes,
Thor-like,
he rises above my charade
to catch my being through the bars.

The birds above him float like
shadows in the rising heat.
He is pulsing to the flutter of wings.
Our lives, his, mine, a scroll
unwinding.

I kneel to him in his short history
and offer him mine,
longer, formed of earth and people,
riding the marble lions of my youth,
in heat, always, seeking and giving love.

A three-legged dog topples over
and I hear only his breathing.

Venice

A tenor's aging voice is clipped in the night air,
a woman's arm reaches out to close her shutters.

The gondolier toe pushes against a wall in a cross canal,
a faceless tableau of people strings along a bridge,

and they stand and we sit in the midst of ambivalence,
tourists and romantics caught up in the cadence of an oar.

Soon the four gondolas merge into the main canal and
we dangle fingers in the velvet water and follow with

our eyes candlelight from the banks of restaurants and
moonlight seeping in and out of richly black clouds.

Entering a cross canal in wide arcs, the gondolas fall
into a single line and head back to the docking area.

In the shadows a tin cup sits on the dock where we
will alight, reminding us that our ambivalence lies

somewhere between our hold on what makes life
magical and what the exchange rate of the Euro is.

Bird Watching

It appeared majestically in my view,
walking tall, purposefully south on
9N,
straddling the double yellow lines,
hypnotically heading south.

The first car passed over him and I
watched for feathers to fly.
Instead he blew several feet and with
panache he continued his walk.

The second car roared over him,
anchoring and then blowing him away,
like fluff in the wind.

A truck's after wind sent him tumbling
up the road, feathers in place,
a plume defying the wind.

He passed out of my sight, still heading
south, flying by now, I hoped, or reaching
the side of the road;

I passed him while going for the mail
one morning,
his body still perfectly formed.
He had worked his way to the bushes,
pointing south on 9N.

The Eve of Hunting Season

Across the road clothes wind wave to us in autumn.
Trees blush in their final splendor and winter birds
huddle in evergreens on a far hill.

Bound hay like loaves of bread are scattered in the
fields and a mouse races in the shadow of an owl.
A gray barn hugs the side of a hill and lets sunshine
enter from wide open doors at either end.

Huge brown and white cattle nose their way to
a muddy trail which is locked in their memory.
They look at passing cars with indifference and
stand seemingly in awe of a rusted, thin barbed
wire fence following the contours of a rolling
pasture.

In another woods posted signs from left over
hunting seasons bleed into the trees or hang
from nails like antique parchment.

The newer signs assert themselves boldly on
old trees, flattened by wind and nail.
They are lined up in rows, mathematically
distant from each other like sentinels.

A white tailed deer with a keen sense of the
turn of weather, pads gently over the ground,
ears up and legs primed for the race. His genes
possess escape and death, the shattered silence
reverberates off mountains, and he feels the
stinging song of blood or the gentle ooze
flowing from a bullet just inches off angle.

In their red and orange vests, the hunters practice,
their genes stirring, rifles lifted, and rhythmically
tear apart the stuffed deer not far from where they
will hang this year's bounty.

The blood will disappear by the third spring rain,
and the gene pool will advance to a new generation.

Joggers

Winter had combed the trees and
I watch him float through the
branches like air and slow dance
his way down the hill.

His dog stops to paw at the
blue bins overloaded with jars,
bottles, flattened boxes, magazines,
and newspapers. He sniffs at the
tangle of orange rinds let loose by
crows, coffee grains spilling from
the side of a white bag, egg shells
dripping juices from breakfast, ends
of toast, and smelly slippers, double-
wrapped.

The jogger runs in place and whistles
for his dog to leave his feast and feast
instead on the upcoming turn in the
road and the mysteries beyond.

The dog looks up for a second and
then proceeds to have slippers with
his breakfast.

Garbage day is a mystery he has
unraveled many jogs ago.

At the Very Feel of Night

Bats behind my shutters twitch in their sleep,

salivating in their dreams,

their droppings falling like pellets upon the porch.

At the very feel of night they inch up the shutters,

paying homage to their instincts,

then they beat their wings furiously,

carrying the night with them,

stabbing the darkness here and there,

disappearing, appearing in the moon's light,

silhouetted against the night sky,

zig zagging, stabbing the night,

wiping out generations of insects as

quietly as this.

Country Life

The slow hissing of leaves releases fall,
the sun turns beach sand to glass,
the man in the moon is pocked-marked,
fish swim through the heron's legs,
the woodpile undulates through the winter,
electric fences spill their juice,
animals parallel play,
barbed-wire fences stretch wearily,
a truck is buried like an old carcass,
the dirt road falls in on itself,
taxes are due on the 15th,
a school bus wades through mud,
holiday lights dim in the off-season,
the trailer park drives away,
town meeting is sold at auction,
sap drips from old wounds,
frost heaves appear like miniature quakes,
the owl spits out feather and bone,
the developer calculates population
density and income per capita,
the planning committee meets Wednesday,
the same day as garbage pickup for the southern
section of town.

Philosophers on Sunday

Aristotle's idea of happiness was to curl
up with a good syllogism.
Plato ran a charter school for Philosopher-
Kings.
Socrates argued with himself and
examined his wife.
Descartes never thought he doubted
and never doubted that he thought.
Locke doodled on his blank slate.
Schopenhauer had a habit of drinking
too much wine and bringing on a migraine.
The hedonists ate, drank, and went looking
for burial plots.
Nietzsche sewed a big S on all of his undershirts.
Emerson consistently warred against consistency.
St. Paul complained that money was the
root of all evil and skipped the Sunday offering.
Pope made sure he checked his answers twice.
Rousseau believed that might does not make
right. Sunday he healed.
Heidegger and Hegel saw truth differently and
declared Sunday off limits if the truth be told.
Kant defied his conscience and slept late.
Mill believed that everyone was equal except on
the buffet line in the parish hall.
Hobbs dead-bolted himself in the house, lowered
all the shades, and did not feed his pet terrier.

Throughout recorded history Sunday has provided
a challenge to the most learned among us.

Digging the Pond

The derrick traumatizes the earth by displacing rocks
the size of large fish, the ground dirt tosses and turns
in its sleep, a neighbor I have never seen before
appears high on the hill, a dot beneath the
row of trees, drawn by curiosity,
satisfied by reasons only he knows, he departs
as quietly as he came.

Metal tracks move over the ground,
The operator builds the sides of the pond, rubbing the
backside of the giant hand gently against the incline,
the beast cupping in its palm rivulets of water
spilling like capillaries, earth tears for the scarred
lawn, waiting to heal.

The pond slowly fills, asserting itself upon the landscape.
In the spring, arriving like silent refugees, frogs begin their
discordant call to life. Koi fish are dropped into the
water and shatter into color. The heron becomes a
statue on the lawn and the snake, too, waits for the feast.
Algae grows from habit in the murky water.

In winter the snow melt glaciers over the grass and down
the driveway, soon the ice reappears in clumps and the
children slow walk over the moon-lit surface.

A mud cast covers the frogs,
fish hover between water and ice,
and the heron leaves fossil prints upon the clay bottom.

A bench is privy to the change of seasons and hunches
over in obeisance to the pull of nature.

Musk Ox

Musk Ox form a O when the
perception of danger lurks.
The circle breathes as one
in the frozen air, nostrils
steam as the hair mats down
and the heads bend at an angle.

The O tightens of its own accord,
the perceived danger is somewhere
out there. The wind plays a mournful
tune, snow blinds the eye, and clouds
imprison the moon.

The night moves slowly towards the
dawn, animal heat melts the snow, and
strength stains the landscape. When the
perceived danger leaves the collective
instinct, the circle imperceptively widens
until each single heartbeat is restored,
each beast raises its head, and, if as on cue,
the pack fans out in all directions.
Danger disappears into the light of morning.

On Waking Up All Over the World

People wake up to their own rhythm, all over the world.
 Women sweep and men with hoses muscle debris too
    heavy for the broom.
Huddled on benches like sculpture, old men select
    memories of youth.

Men and women ritually move from one apparatus to
    another in the twilight
before dawn, their breath spilling out strength, their
    thoughts taking on
delusions of grandeur in the park.

A young women behind a hotel front desk is startled from
    sleep,
dogs shake off dew and flowers coyly spread open,
seducing the camera's eye.

Cathedral bells do not waken the woman with the twisted
    body who
sleeps on the steps while the balloon man maneuvers the
    wind,
people standing like clothes racks in a mall wait for the bus.

School children in uniforms of brown or black or blue,
move through the park as quietly as ants, their backpacks
    worn
with a gentle elegance.

Elder Hostel guests litter the hotel lobby with their luggage,
memories of the continental breakfast giving way to
    thoughts
of lunch. The tour guide charms them with ritualistic
    humor.

A boy of six or seven stakes out his territory in front of a
    bank,
his assortment of rags and brushes neatly stored, his
    polishes
waiting for his stained fingers, making a living a shoe at a
    time.

Women breast feed their children in cubicles still filled with
yesterday's air, wearing their village colors,
waiting for tourists who bargain down.

Men carrying machetes walk downhill for the daily wood
    load,
their upright bodies throwing straight shadows before them,
towards evening, they stoop uphill, life burdened.

The markets aroma the air with fruits and vegetables,
in church the crossed foot of Christ is worn with kisses,
teenage secrets unravel with laughter.

Mopeds awaken the slumber of the catacombs,
the concierge circles the route to the Vatican,
on cue, pigeons and national birds assert their
    independence.

In my hotel room, I close the curtain, cataloguing my
    mental
notes and allowing intermission to render judgment
on what I just saw and what I will see. Breakfast awaits.

On Taking My Daughter to Have Her Ear Lanced

My hands pressed her shoulders into the table.

She spilled the pain by turning her head until the leather
hissed.

A single moth attracted by the light above the table,
danced in her eyes.

He poured sleep into her and she pushed against me and
then

vanished like Raggedy Ann into a sea of clothes.

He lanced the ear; she grew hard again.

Her eyes caught the moth.

"You were asleep," I said.

Garage Sale

"You have to turn the head by hand," she said. "It still
    works."
I nodded and placed the musical lamp on an old book
    case.
A single note hung in the air.

A rimless tire balanced itself against a wall,
spider webs from another season stretched lazily in its
    hollow.
"The other tire wore out," she said. "Must not have
    rotated it."

I ran my hand along the railing of a crib.
"That crib will take more kids. Takes more than two or
    three
babies to wear them out."

She pointed to a mattress. "We have been sleeping on
    that for
over thirty years. Still has some good years left."

"That sled just needs new runners and it will be good as
    new."
"Is there anything you had in mind?"
"Not really," I said.

She turned quickly.
"You have to turn the head by hand," she said. "It still
    works."
A single note hung in the air.

Encounter

Tapping the glass,
from back to back,
from side to side,
landing on the headrest
behind my head,
commotion in my ears,
nervous energy expended
in my swipes at it,
an inordinate fear
staining my shirt.

Later, it lights
upon the glass to my left,
the buzzing taking on new
resonance,
I slowly lower the window,
and when there is more wind
than window,
the bee is away
with no look back,
no more conditioned air
to proscribe its time and space,
no more instinctive search for
freedom.

Relief toes the gas pedal,
speed becomes my sanctuary.

Homily

Temper the brimstone, give me fire.
Save your eye contact for me,
limit your eloquence to my life,
my soul is needy, my ears await
your words and His. I am alone in
the pew, incense lingers in my memory,
candle light conquers my darkness,
song resurrects my memories,

Your gentle kiss summons my attention,
my body leans into your voice,
you speak to my needs,
it hurts to concentrate so hard,
the wound is opened, the balm is applied,
I whistle quietly when you finish.

It is at the Sign of Peace that I am most
aware of my neediness, hands are thrust
at me, I feel the presence of others.

Home has a new address.

Life on the Second Floor

Ice, shaped like picks, hung down below the
boarded window on the second floor.
An old wreath faded and hardly round
drooped in front of a shade that didn't
care about the sun any more;

A head peeked from behind the shade
and moist breath blew miniature clouds
of air on to the back of the windowpane;
the head pulled back suddenly, as if
unaccustomed to light and the sounds
of life on the dizzy street below;

A railroad yard lay still and children ran
across the tracks without looking and
made it to the other side, alive. The head
appeared again and cocked an ear to hear
if the 6:02 was coming down the tracks.

This time it stayed a little longer and a
heart beat a little stronger as the whistle
of the train warned everyone to get out
of the way and little kids turned and ran
and one of the ice picks clicked off and
the wreath rounded and shaped the head
and the train came in on time.

The old lady smiled and set the table for
two.

School House

You are standing by the window,
sun spilling over your shoulders,
watching wild turkeys neck-walk
across the grass and behind an old
stone foundation where children
went to school, desks once anchored
where the turkeys appear and disappear
in the heavy grass.

Children leap into recess, hide
and seek scampers behind rocks and trees,
the turkeys with bobbing heads ride the
grass, a bell is choked by decades of dirt
and fails to signal the end of recess.

You are afraid to move too quickly,
the mother turkey stretches her neck
to the fullest, the babies seeking her
shadow, circle her and move trackless
in the deep grass,

I whisper lunch to you,
once again, lunch,
but you disappear deeper into the sunlight,
deeper into recess, closing your lunchbox
with a tiny click, letting me know that you
have eaten your fill.

The Woodshed in Winter

The woodshed has a randomness to it,
the rakes scratch against the metal poles
of a hammock, the grill hunches over in its cover,
a riding mower rises on cinder blocks,
the weed whacker runs out of cutting cord,
the hose piles upon itself in a corner.

And the winter occupants nestle in the insulation,
bird feeders crust with seeds in their sills,
a ladder tip toes towards the loft,
frayed wires hang from the ceiling,
water forms on the window like beads of mercury,
a mole crawls in and out of a whiffle ball, and
a chipmunk proclaims his place with urine.

Wasp hives reveal their secret chambers,
leaves pile up against the door.
I struggle with the rusted lock, fitting in a
litany of keys until the bottom slips d
                                        o
                                        w
                                        n

and I am able to open the door to spring.

The Sunporch

I bring yesterday's coals back to life
in the second day break after the twilight
rain. I wonder if that plane will finish
ahead of the clouds? The rugs on the line
hang like flags, changing colors as the
shadows quicken over them.

The grill is old and wet and tips on one
caster. I am the falconer with my glove
moving the coals around, training pigeons
in my sleep, watching them fly away.
Where is the water tower? Why does it
disappear in summer when I need it?
Why does the grass grow best under
the sunporch?

There are more things, Horatio.
I'll kill that praying mantis when
no one is looking. It will not die until
it does what it is supposed to do.
Now and then a bird drowns catching
fish too heavy to carry. Its bones drift
in the wake of ships, lonely driftwood,
wind blowing through and sand.
In the forest at night, color stops.
The tree which bursts to flames between
two rocks spills its leaves like wine.

Through wispy smoke I see the swing set
climbing the stairs on cement feet.

My biography will at best record those
things people could see.

The Death of the Last Whale

Three tons of tongue lolling

in its mouth, its body too big,

its lungs too small for its own

good, its song caught up in

sonar.

                         Unmerciful blips on a screen,

a holding pattern in water,

a shaft of light and only itself

upon the volcanic rock.

Generations drying up upon

the rock, hissing steam,

fossilized, and he, himself,

moving forward in the darkness,

without shadow, tail striking at

nothing, heart pumping blood

strangely, organically, without

passion, without fire.

                And around him blood, warm

against his body, drifting, only

a rumor of life, death upon the

marble surface, and he with

only a dark stare, hollow-eyed,

breaking the water ahead.

                Inside him an explosion of heart,

the power of tons of heart,

ramming against skeletal ships,

mountains waiting to be born,

anything with a shadow, ramming,

bursting, sending wood and stone

everywhere, and heart.

                Stretching out to speak of freedom,

the lover gone from the bed,

freedom to thrash, to think quiet

thoughts, to feel one's presence

intimately, totally.

But then the dreaded freedom

breaks cold and wet upon the

skin, dying a little like a lamp in

sunlight.

Someone, perhaps is drowning in the

Sea of Tranquility.

Resurrect him. Lift off.

In his life lightning is striking with

more regularity.

He has learned to turn the hour glass,

to stay alone a little longer,

to fake a stone when life is too much.

Above again, lightning rods poised,

picking up the rope, passing it

through fingers, wetting it down,

their nakedness a torch in the sun,

they can feel the ancient song in the

throat, see the water blown through

the tomb, alone in its magnificence,

transfigured beyond all hope and

time, the last of the great whales.

He must not go down. Faster,

faster, a race to be gods, a race of

gods to be laid low, to be ridden no

more, for the sake of God to be put

out of its misery!

Strike! Strike! Strike!

Wet the rope you fool!

It must not break.

Closer! Closer!

Again! Again!

Strike!

Hit! Let out the rope. He will ride us

for awhile and we will ride him.

The sky is blood shot and his death is

warm, and good, and final.

5:37 P.M. E.S.T.

Flight 1437

From my window seat I can see the world in flight,
shedding skin like a snake, the land becoming water,
the water land, cows becoming boulders, and cows
again, checkerboards of grass tumbling wildly on,
moving under the chicken coop poised on cinder
blocks, smelling of corn and feathers, and farmer's
sweat. There is the drama of the dead fox and the
house undoing itself from the basement to the roof,
and an egg wrapped in grass turning to stone, waiting
to be skimmed over water in a pond.
Where the grass stops, there is earth hardening below.

Starting the descent, I see a scarecrows's hat propped
against the ribs of a wagon resting like a lazy buffalo,
straps flicking for flies, rain spilling out of its sides,
the ribs expanding and contracting with the movement
of the earth.

Further on, canteens are spilling out dust, hanging in
trees like ghosts. The shadow of a train runs out and
the rails lie quietly in grass. A windmill turns in
reluctant half circles, falling in and out of light, mice
tucked away, their metabolism quickening to an idea,
their simple bones caught up in hunger.

The landing is smooth. I hear the clicks of the seat
belts opening before we have come to the gate. And
cell phones are thumbed into life. I am the last to
deplane, wondering if I will ever become accustomed
to eye level again.

Columbia University in the Sixties

Jutting gargoyles no longer
choking on water, no longer
screeching through the centuries,
rust down their gullets and
bronze with their secrets;

Latin phrases unread by
students, burn the air
with their truths;

Marble heads staring into elevator
shafts lick cigarette ash from their
lips and blacken in their place;

Iron fences stand bow-legged in
grass and their sun shadows
imprison strawmen hanged and
burned;

The bell in the tower stirs,
the cemetery awakens to marching feet,
slumbering bones clack together
and push aside stones epitaphed
by chisel and weather;

The marble heads are blungeoned
and fall into baskets, grass is trampled,
metal bars are stretched,
strawmen scream, and gargoyles spit
blood over sanded walls like vintage
wine whose year has come.

Richardson Cemetery

At night when the loudest sound comes from my
eyes opening, when my dreams end as suddenly,
I reach for a pad on the night table and scribble,
"flags popping up like lilies in a Civil War
Cemetery on a country road."

Later, awake and asleep, I hear my shoes
stepping on last fall's leaves, I see a mole
emerging from spring grass near the edge
of the cemetery. The stone engraver's art
is lost to weather and my fingers play upon
each stone.

The children are easy to find, tiny slabs poking
up like shoots of spring, scattered here and there
among the larger stones, some of those split
jaggedly or lying like fallen towers. In my half
sleep I mingle with the mourners who rain tiny
pebbles upon the casket and with the wife who
places a rose where the heart would be.

Richardson Cemetery awakens with color on
Memorial Day when the earth warms once again.
Taps play distantly in my uneasy dreams.

Attention Deficit Disorder

You see me staring in space, listening to the
distant elevator slam to a halt, the waves
chasing the sandpipers, the caterpillar
escaping the cocoon, the wings of the
butterfly barely moving the air,
an egg cracking with new life, the fetus
tapping its legs in the womb.

I am looking and listening to new life and
I can take you to sights and sounds you have
never known and meanings you have never thought,
or tell you what color car belongs to every
teacher and who was late on Tuesday if
you ask.

I ask only to be new born.

The Search for the Ivory-Billed Woodpecker

The silent opened-mouth water moccasin guards the
    secret well,
lurking like a large S in the bayou swamp.
Oil drips from the chain saw and percolates deep inside
    the ground,
the dust flakes of a million trees harden like coal,
the waters swell and constrict with the whims of weather.
Trees tilt at different angles, rising out of the water,
more dead than alive.
Beaver dams shatter like pick-up-sticks.

Endangered gives way to extinct.
Semantics plays a part.
Extinction is our word for what was.
What was now exists in shadows,
in silence, in a wished-for echo,
in the never-more of sightings.
Forever gone, forever sought.
The looking for and the looking at
tangle in a war of juxtaposition,
but not once does he think of us
or hide from us.
It is just that our camera pivots too slowly,
our sound system is all chatter.

It is there in the underside of a wing,
in the length of its bill,
in the size of its body,

in a nesting hole,
in a open wound where the grubs fester,
in a yellowing photograph,
in a grainy film,
stuffed and mounted on the mantle.
An Ivory-bill hangs on wires in a museum exhibit,
another is posed pecking outside a nesting hole.
The bird meticulously spreads his legs,
talons grip the side of the tree,
red-tufted, determined, unflinching,
bill poised for grubs, on the brink of decision.

Rite of Initiation

He measured each step,
gagging on the darkness,
his giant thighs cracking
open with each branch.
In his gym shorts, he met
the night and beat on it,
kicking it, pushing it back,
hearing it breathing harder
against every pore.
His own voice heaved him
against a tree and it crashed
under his weight. He lay
in its noise, having discovered
Truth.

The darkness came in waves,
and he lifted it with his
shoulders, knees tucked
against his chest, his body
outlined by sweat, until
it flattened him with the
weight of mountains.
He awoke hungry and anxious
for his mother.
She called to him and he headed
for home.

He fell, not knowing bottom,
and reconsidered his entire life.

The City

A spirit moves through the streets
and hovers low over the puffs of smoke
coming from sewer covers in winter.

Fire escapes creak under the weight
of snow and await the thaw.
The spirit ascends slippery steps.

The roof we climbed covered with
blisters of tar in summer is soothed by the
gentle pat of snow.
It sleeps undisturbed by the
spirit.

And the new people in old kitchens
are drawn to leaded window ledges
by the sound of chains
moving over snowy roads.

The spirit gets caught up in weather
and rains on melancholy lives.

Tarred and Feathered

An Irish girl is accused of flirting with a British soldier in
Northern Ireland.
Her head is shaved and tar is smeared on.

She

                                                              Feels

The

                        Feathers

                                                              One

            By

                                                          One

They Are Your Children. And Mine

They have the battle of Lexington on their laps,
cradling matchstick forts and tin soldiers who
march and drum to the rhythm of the bus,
lacrosse sticks held high, hockey sticks
searching for the elusive puck, bowling balls
wrapped like giant eggs in cotton, water pistols
leaking in their pockets, firecrackers spilling
powder into jacket linings, poison pen letters
yellowing in their jeans, gum wrappers meta-
morphosizing into bracelets, magic markers the
color of graffiti, and an occasional book to
betray their destination.

Who are they? They are your children. And
Mine. They look like us. They share our names.
They carry our hopes and their dreams on
shoulders more than a boy's, less than a man's,
more than a girl's, less than a woman's.

They can bully and brag and be cruel. They can
cry over a rumor, laugh uncontrollably over
nothing, smile to cover their hurt, and
amaze us at how quickly they can move from
one emotion to another.

They run instead of walk, shout instead of whisper,
forget their lunch, their money, their homework,
all too often. The lost and found table groans
under the weight of boots, sneakers, pocketbooks,
retainers in plastic cups, sweaters, gym shorts,
baseball gloves, jackets, notebooks, textbooks,
but not one single example of that relic from our
day-the earmuff. (And they say times haven't
changed.)

They carry enough collective wire in their mouths
to tilt the world several more degrees off its axis.
They can find a contact lens within a radius of a
thousand feet and not be able to avoid that one
wet spot in an empty hallway. They can sit
absolutely silent in a crowded gymnasium when
one of their peers attempts a dangerous stunt on
the uneven bars. They can cook and sew, publish
a newspaper, put together a yearbook, handle tools

dangerous enough for a grown-up, make the honor
roll, come to school with a cold, catch the measles,
lose their first fight, have their first boyfriend or
girlfriend, dissect their first anything, grow inches,
gain pounds, and leave in two years with a different
body from the one in which they entered. They
spend their junior high years shedding the imposters
who changed every second, every minute, every hour,
every day, every month, searching constantly for
their real selves.

They do get tired and hurt, and they need a kind word
or look from us more often than you think. They will
walk for any charity, bike in any bike-a-thon, drink more
water than a camel, dance themselves into shin splints,
and then come to physical education with a medical
excuse. They will eat a potato chip and Dorito® lunch,
topped off by an Italian ice and a Twinkie® and six
containers of chocolate milk. They store enough
sandwiches in their lockers to feed a continent, and
they prove without a doubt that peanut butter does
turn into stone when tucked away in a locker for six
months.

They play for our athletic teams in rain and snow,
wallow in mud, and break bones-all in front of a
very few people. They can play music with a talent
beyond their years. They fit everything in among

orthodontist appointments, religion classes, piano lessons, ballet lessons, gymnastic lessons, ice skating lessons, measles, mumps, chicken pox, family quarrels, family celebrations, and homework. They are not made of steel. They have serious illnesses, spend time in the hospital, and suffer from perhaps the most serious ailment for all adolescents, a broken heart. They experience family discord, family illness, and death in the family. They find comfort in a friend, support from peers, and we hope, love and understanding from us.

Who are they? They are your children. And mine. They look like us. They share our names. And they spend most of their lives away from our direct influence. But our indirect influence in the form of directions planted and love given will remain with them to comfort and guide them for the rest of their days. The greatest sign of a successful teacher or parent is not what the student or child did while in the classroom, or in the home, but what he or she does with his or her life when we are a memory or phone call away. May that memory never be too faint or that phone too busy to answer.

Paul Paparella (1979) "They Are Your Children and Mine," Educational Leadership, 37, 2: 169-170. Reprinted with permission of the Association of Supervision and Curriculum Development. Copy 1979 by ASCD. All rights reserved.

Printed in the United States
203719BV00001B/193-294/A